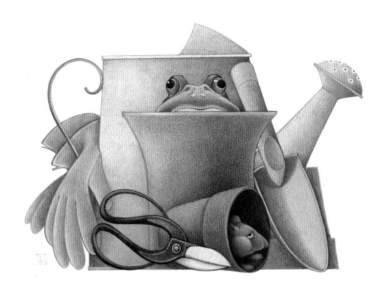

A Gardener's Calendar & Journal
Artwork by Linnea Riley

Distributed by The Madison Park Group, Inc.
1407 Eleventh Avenue
Seattle, Washington 98122
www.linneadesign.com

ISBN 978-0-9842519-0-2
Manufactured in China

No two gardens are the same. No two days are the same in one garden.

– English gardener, Hugh Johnson

A Gardener's Calendar & Journal

Here is a calendar-journal to record a year in the biography of your garden. Plan your plantings and prunings, record your garden's bounty and blooms. Keep an annual record so you will be able to compare your results with those of previous years' and check this year's temperature highs and lows with last year's. Record your growing successes and inspirational plant pairings. Make notes of reminder for timely garden chores throughout the seasons. Use the grid to design your garden; and keep track of suppliers, horticultural helpers, plant tags and instructions with this book's special pages and bound-in envelopes. Include a sketch…maybe a snapshot or two, to remember some of the beautiful moments in your garden.

This journal belongs to:

_____

Year:

_____

January

first week

second week

third week

fourth week

Temperature high/low

1	2	3	4	5	6	7	8	9	10	11	12	13	14	15	16	17	18	19	20	21	22	23

24 25 26 27 28 29 30 31

Plant Variety	Date Planted	Source

My green thumb came only as a result of mistakes I made while learning to see things from the plant's point of view.

– H. Fred Ale

February

first week

second week

third week

fourth week

Temperature high/low

1	2	3	4	5	6	7	8	9	10	11	12	13	14	15	16	17	18	19	20	21	22	23

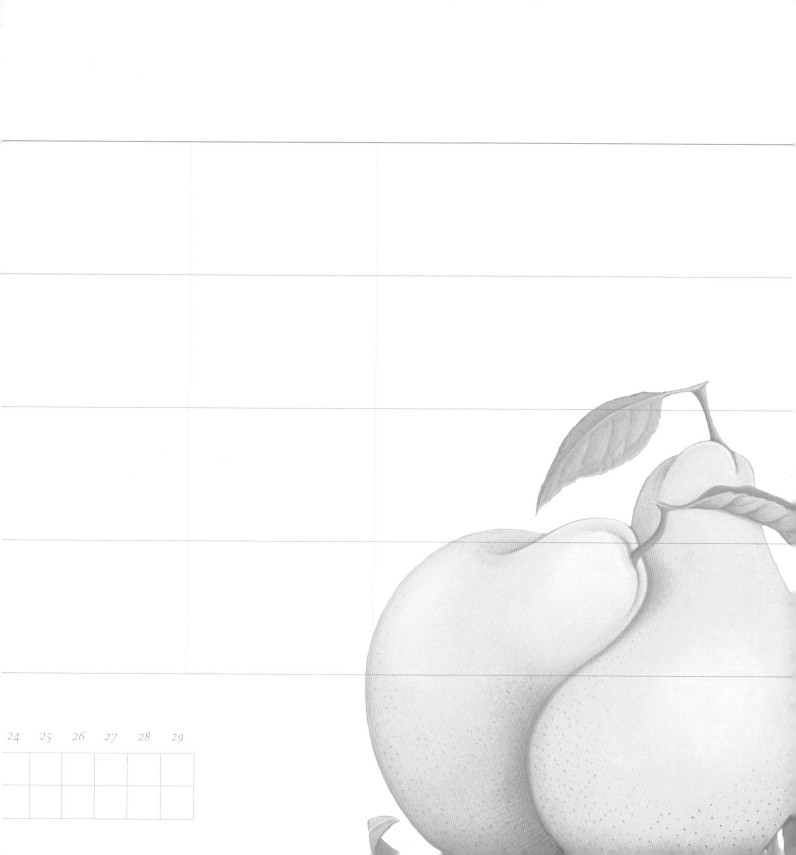

24   25   26   27   28   29

Plant Variety	Date Planted	Source

- Columnar / upright Juniper or cedar (bluish gray · silver). check size. May have two or one depending on size.
- Fence ideas: Jacks Rustic Wood fences in Niles / Fenceworks / Guyon 41 Fences
- Florist Water base spraypaint — Michaels. Spring Tree wrap · chalet   b. get sample for Lake Front
- Rock from Buy the yard · Cedar Mulch April
- Get new grass to grow
- Plant lettuce seeds

One of the most delightful things about a garden is the anticipation it provides.

– W. E. Johns

March

first week

second week

third week

fourth week

Temperature high/low

1	2	3	4	5	6	7	8	9	10	11	12	13	14	15	16	17	18	19	20	21	22	23

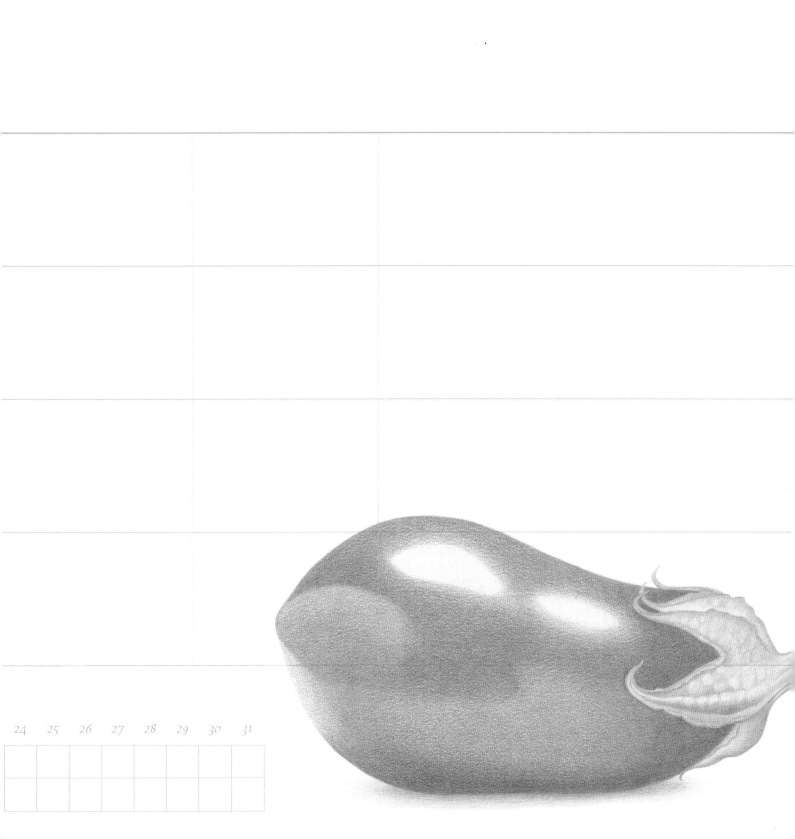

24   25   26   27   28   29   30   31

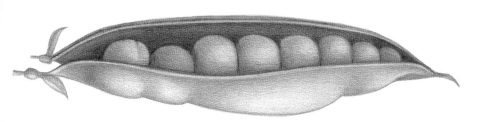

Plant Variety	Date Planted	Source

Green fingers are the extension of a verdant heart.

– Russell Page

April

first week

second week

third week

fourth week

Temperature high/low

1	2	3	4	5	6	7	8	9	10	11	12	13	14	15	16	17	18	19	20	21	22	23

24 25 26 27 28 29 30

Plant Variety	Date Planted	Source

April Notes

The best fertilizer is the gardener's shadow.

– Author Unknown

May

first week

second week

third week

fourth week

Temperature high/low

1	2	3	4	5	6	7	8	9	10	11	12	13	14	15	16	17	18	19	20	21	22	23

24 25 26 27 28 29 30 31

Plant Variety	Date Planted	Source

May Notes

June

first week

second week

third week

fourth week

Temperature high/low

1	2	3	4	5	6	7	8	9	10	11	12	13	14	15	16	17	18	19	20	21	22	23

24   25   26   27   28   29   30

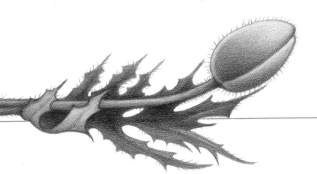

Plant Variety	Date Planted	Source

June Notes

In gardens, beauty is a by-product. The main business is sex and death.

– Sam Llewelyn

July

first week

second week

third week

fourth week

Temperature high/low

1	2	3	4	5	6	7	8	9	10	11	12	13	14	15	16	17	18	19	20	21	22	23

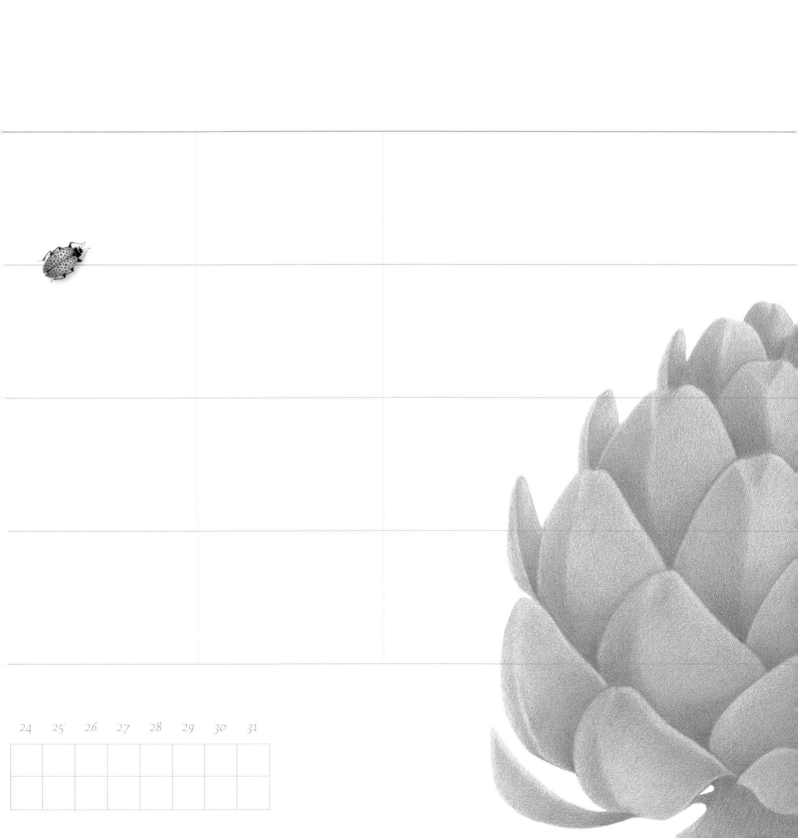

24 25 26 27 28 29 30 31

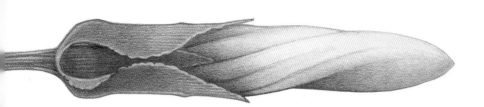

Plant Variety	Date Planted	Source

July Notes

God made rainy days so gardeners could get the housework done.

– Author Unknown

August

first week

second week

third week

fourth week

Temperature high/low

1	2	3	4	5	6	7	8	9	10	11	12	13	14	15	16	17	18	19	20	21	22	23

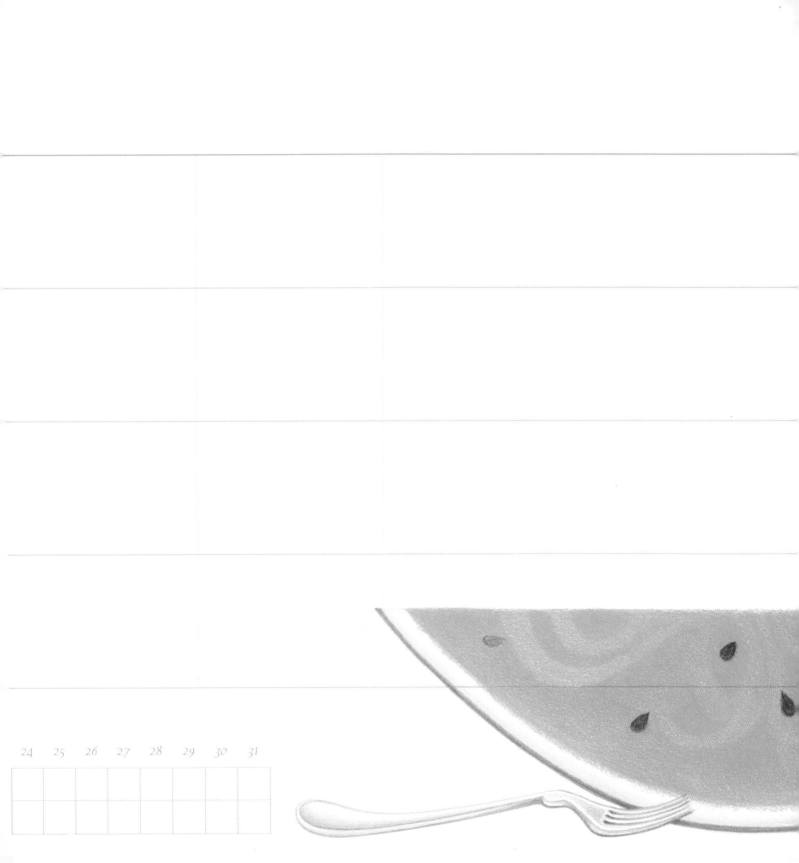

24　25　26　27　28　29　30　31

Plant Variety	Date Planted	Source

Unemployment is capitalism's way of getting you to plant a garden.

– Orson Scott Card

September

first week

second week

third week

fourth week

Temperature high/low

1	2	3	4	5	6	7	8	9	10	11	12	13	14	15	16	17	18	19	20	21	22	23

24 25 26 27 28 29 30

Plant Variety	Date Planted	Source

You can bury a lot of trouble digging in the dirt.

– Author Unknown

October

first week

second week

third week

fourth week

Temperature high/low

1	2	3	4	5	6	7	8	9	10	11	12	13	14	15	16	17	18	19	20	21	22	23

24   25   26   27   28   29   30   31

Plant Variety	Date Planted	Source

October Notes

Gardens are a form of autobiography.

– Sydney Eddison

November

first week

second week

third week

fourth week

Temperature high/low

1	2	3	4	5	6	7	8	9	10	11	12	13	14	15	16	17	18	19	20	21	22	23

24   25   26   27   28   29   30

Plant Variety	Date Planted	Source

November Notes

A garden is never so good as it will be next year.

– Thomas Cooper

December

first week

second week

third week

fourth week

Temperature high/low

1	2	3	4	5	6	7	8	9	10	11	12	13	14	15	16	17	18	19	20	21	22	23

24	25	26	27	28	29	30	31

Plant Variety	Date Planted	Source

December Notes

I think that if ever a mortal heard the voice of God it would be in a garden at the cool of the day.

– F. Frankfort Moore

Laying out grounds may be considered a liberal art, in some sort like poetry and painting. – William Wordsworth

Nurseries, Seed Companies, Landscapers, Arborists

When weeding, the best way to make
sure you are removing a weed and not
a valuable plant is to pull on it. If it
comes out of the ground easily, it is
a valuable plant.

Author Unknown